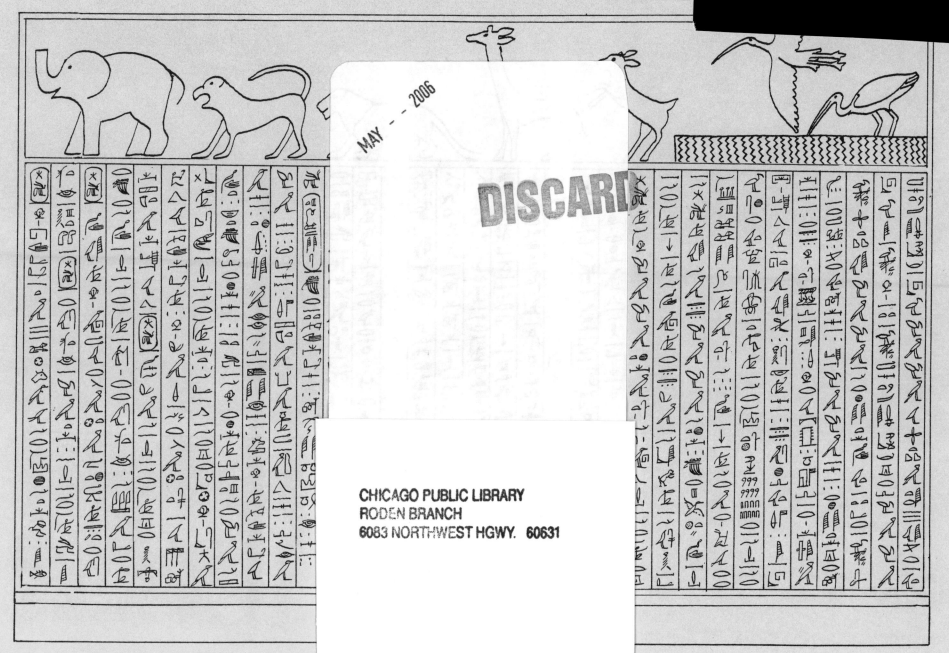

P9-CCU-874

MAY - - 2006

DISCARD

CHICAGO PUBLIC LIBRARY
RODEN BRANCH
6083 NORTHWEST HGWY.   60631

ALONG THE NILE RIVER, the ibis bird uses its long, curved bill to search for food. In ancient Egypt, the ibis was sacred to the god Thoth , who also had a long, curved bill. But instead of searching for food, Thoth searched for knowledge. According to legend, Thoth gave the ancient Egyptians pictures to use for writing. With the gift of writing, the Egyptians became seekers of knowledge, too.

For three thousand years, the Egyptians wrote about their world, covering their temples with words, filling their libraries with books. Then invaders came and destroyed Egypt, and the pictures called hieroglyphs were forgotten.

3200 B.C.

À la mémoire de mon cher ami Harry G. Lewis,
1914–1980

2000 B.C.

Seeker *of* Knowledge

The Man Who Deciphered Egyptian Hieroglyphs

James Rumford

HOUGHTON MIFFLIN COMPANY ♘ BOSTON

1790 A.D.

R0406816283

CHICAGO PUBLIC LIBRARY
RODEN BRANCH
6083 NORTHWEST HGWY. 60631

There is a jumping,
free-spirited kid goat
in the Egyptian word
"imagine."

In 1790, a French boy named Jean-François Champollion was born  .

When he was seven, his older brother told him about General Napoleon, the great leader of France, who was in Egypt uncovering the past.

"Someday I'll go to Egypt, too!" Jean-François told his brother as he sat spellbound, imagining himself with Napoleon, making his own discoveries  .

There is a sharp-eyed
ibis bird in the word
"discover."

When Jean-François was eleven, he went to school in the city of Grenoble. There, his brother took him to meet a famous scientist who had been in Egypt with Napoleon.

The scientist's house was filled with Egyptian treasures. Each one captured the boy's imagination.

"Can anyone read their writing?" asked Jean-François.

"No. No one," the scientist replied.

"Then I will one day," said Jean-François, and he left the house full of enthusiasm, sure that he would be the first to discover the key to Egyptian hieroglyphs.

There is a long-necked, far-seeing giraffe in "predict."

Back home, his brother helped him get down all the books they had on Egypt. On moonlit nights, Jean-François stayed up reading long after he should have been asleep.

His brother nicknamed him "the Egyptian" and bought him notebooks. Jean-François filled them with hieroglyphs. There were prowling lions , angry monkeys, trumpeting elephants, and sharp-eyed ibis birds with their long, curved bills. He could not read the Egyptian words, but he dreamed that one day he would, as he sailed up the Nile.

Jean-François had a favorite animal. It was the lion because there was one in his name: JEAN-FRANÇOIS CHAMPOL**LION**.

The Rosetta Stone: hieroglyphs at the top, a cursive form of hieroglyphs called demotic in the middle, and Greek at the bottom

When Jean-François finished school at sixteen, his brother took him to Paris to meet 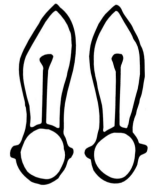 the scholars who were studying a black stone from Rosetta, Egypt. The stone was covered with Egyptian and Greek words and told of a king of Egypt named Ptolemy. By reading the Greek, the scholars hoped to decipher the Egyptian. But the work was difficult—certainly too difficult for a boy—and the scholars turned Jean-François away . They did not see the fire burning bright in his eyes. They did not recognize the genius who had already learned all the known ancient languages. They did not know that he was a seeker of knowledge, one who would not rest until he had found the answer.

There are strongly woven sandals firmly planted on the ground in "never give up."

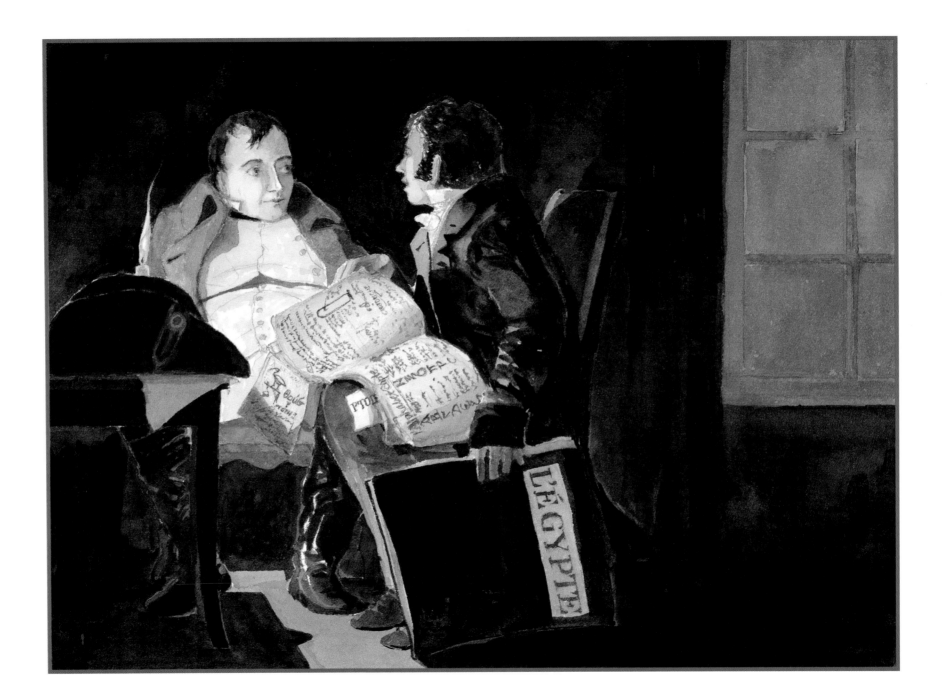

Thothmes (also written Thutmose *or* Thutmosis)*, one of the ancient pharaohs*

Jean-François gathered his notebooks and returned to Grenoble. There he taught school. His students often came to hear him talk about Egypt—her pharaohs and gods and the mysterious writing.

Once, even Napoleon came to Grenoble and sat up all night, listening spellbound as Jean-François told the great man of his dreams.

Napoleon promised to send Jean-François to Egypt when he conquered the world. Napoleon dreamed of glory. Jean-François dreamed of discovery  .

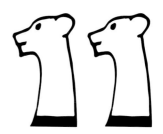

There are two regal, heads-up-high leopards in the word "glory."

Thoth, *one of the ancient gods*

But a few months later, Napoleon was defeated at the Battle of Waterloo. France was now defenseless. Her enemies poured in. They surrounded Grenoble and in the early morning bombarded the city. Jean-François ran  to save his notebooks from the flames.

The people were angry with Napoleon and anyone who knew him. They pointed fingers at Jean-François and called him a traitor. He fled into the woods, leaving his notebooks behind. There he lived like a hunted dog 🐕. It was weeks before it was safe to come out and months before he saw his notebooks again.

There is a roaming, black-as-night jackal in the word "mystery."

*The letter **P** in Ptolemy's name*

*The letter **T** in Ptolemy's name*

During these troubled times, scholars everywhere were racing to solve the mystery of Egyptian writing. Unbelievable things were said. Ridiculous books were written. No one had the answer. Then an Englishman discovered that a few of the hieroglyphs on the Rosetta Stone were letters, and he deciphered King Ptolemy's name. Everyone said that the Englishman would be the first to unlock the door to Egypt's past—everyone except Jean-François $\square\square$.

When Jean-François was thirty, he gathered up his notebooks and left Grenoble. He made his way back to Paris—to his brother.

There is an unblinking crocodile lurking in the word "trouble."

In Paris, Jean-François studied the Rosetta Stone and other inscriptions. He compared the Greek letters with the Egyptian hieroglyphs and herded together his own alphabet of eagles and lions and dark-eyed chicks . But this wonderful list of letters was no help in reading the language. There were too many pictures he did not understand. What to make of a fish with legs , a jackal with wings , or an ibis god with a long, curved bill ? There had to be a link between the pictures and the Egyptian letters. But what was it? Jean-François slept little. He ate almost nothing.

To Jean-François, this was the letter **A**.

And this was the letter **R**.

The letter **W**

Then, on a September morning in 1822, Jean-François found 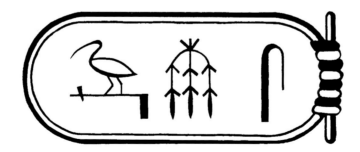 a small package on his doorstep—from a friend in Egypt! In it were the names of pharaohs copied from a temple wall. Each name was a jigsaw puzzle of letters and pictures. Jean-François studied the names and saw the link! The pictures were sounds, too. Not single letters, but syllables, even whole words!

One of the names drew him. It began with the hieroglyph of an old, silent friend perched on a sacred staff ⌇. This was a picture of the god of writing, Thoth, followed by the letters *m* ⋔ and *s* ⌇.

"Thothmes!" Jean-François suddenly exclaimed, and the rushing sound of the pharaoh's name, as if carried on wings across the centuries, filled the room.

The royal cartouche, *or ring of rope, encircling Thothmes's name*

Jean-François raced  down the street to his brother's office. He burst through the door, exclaiming, "I have the key!"

Then he collapsed . He had not eaten. He had not slept. For five days, he lay near death.

There is a blue lotus, its center as bright as the yellow sun, in the word "joy."

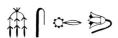

On the fifth day, he awoke. "Pen and paper," he whispered, and he wrote of his discovery to the world.

People all over France celebrated his triumph as Jean-François became the first to translate the ancient writing and open the door to Egypt's past.

There are rippling river waves in the word "Nile."

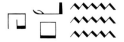

A few years later, the people of France sent Jean-François to Egypt on an expedition to uncover more secrets . He knew Egypt so well in his mind that he felt he was going home. As Jean-François had imagined a thousand times in his dreams, he sailed up the Nile.

Once ashore, he entered the ruins of a temple. A magnificent flock of ibis suddenly rose up from the reeds and took flight.

Below, the ibis saw the seeker of knowledge touch the stone walls.

His fingers dipped into the carved pictures.

He pressed his ear to the stone and listened to the ancient voices.

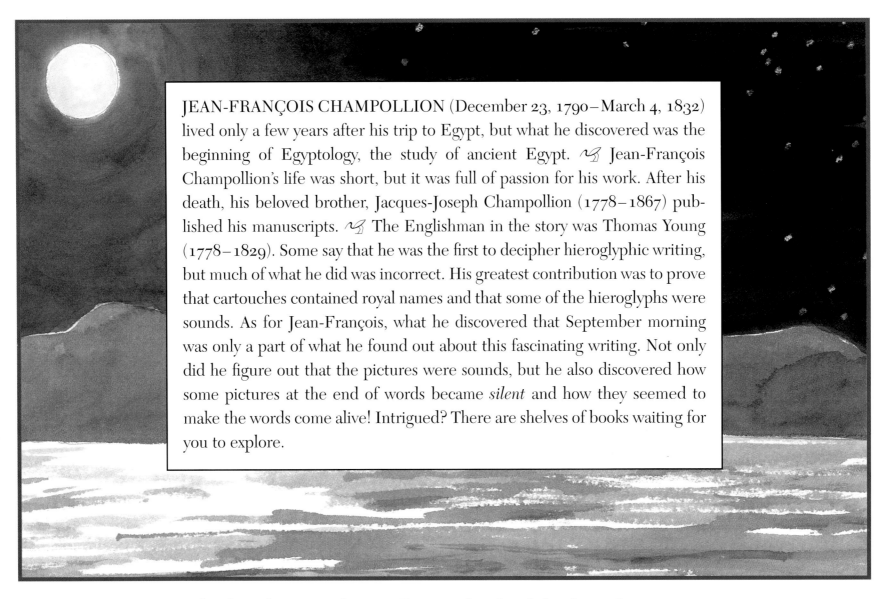

JEAN-FRANÇOIS CHAMPOLLION (December 23, 1790–March 4, 1832) lived only a few years after his trip to Egypt, but what he discovered was the beginning of Egyptology, the study of ancient Egypt. Jean-François Champollion's life was short, but it was full of passion for his work. After his death, his beloved brother, Jacques-Joseph Champollion (1778–1867) published his manuscripts. The Englishman in the story was Thomas Young (1778–1829). Some say that he was the first to decipher hieroglyphic writing, but much of what he did was incorrect. His greatest contribution was to prove that cartouches contained royal names and that some of the hieroglyphs were sounds. As for Jean-François, what he discovered that September morning was only a part of what he found out about this fascinating writing. Not only did he figure out that the pictures were sounds, but he also discovered how some pictures at the end of words became *silent* and how they seemed to make the words come alive! Intrigued? There are shelves of books waiting for you to explore.

The pharaohs' names that Jean-François deciphered that September morning came from the temple at Abu Simbel, which he visited several years later. The last night Jean-François spent there was filled with moonlight.

To give you a taste of what lies ahead, here is a simple Egyptian word: ⌑ ⌋ ⌇. This word means "ibis." The first two hieroglyphs are the letters *h* and *b*. The picture of the ibis is there to give meaning and a bit of magic to the word. ⌇ No one knows the exact pronunciation. The Egyptians did not write the vowels of their language. If you want to pronounce this word, just for fun, add an *e* and say *heb*. It may sound strange, but, as any dictionary will show you, *heb* is the ancestor of our word "ibis." ⌇ Below are the Egyptian words in this book, each with a simplified pronunciation:

heb, ibis

jehooty, Thoth

mes, born

ib, imagine

gem, discover

sensen, meet

ser, predict

mayee, lion

gef, monkey

aboo, elephant

khenty, sail upstream

meseh, turn away

menredewy, never give up

pehety, glory

[pronunciation unknown], run

weher, dog

seshetet, mystery

afa, trouble

bes, rise

khekh, swift

kher, collapse

swash, celebrate

mesesh, joy

hap, River Nile

The facts in this book are based on a French translation (1983) of H. Hartleben's *Champollion, sein Leben und sein Werk* (1906) and on E. Doblhofer's *Voices in Stone* (1963). The hieroglyphs come from A. Gardiner's *Egyptian Grammar* (1957), E. Budge's *An Egyptian Hieroglyphic Dictionary* (1920), J. & L. Scott's *Egyptian Hieroglyphs for Everyone* (1968), and M. Collier and B. Mandy's *How to Read Egyptian Hieroglyphs* (1998). The hieroglyphs in the text were designed by the author.

Deciphering hieroglyphic writing was difficult work, but it was work that Jean-François loved. His fascination with Egypt began when he was very young. Like you, he had dreams, and he spent his life making his dreams come true.

Copyright © 2000 by James Rumford
All rights reserved. For information about permission to reproduce selections from this book, write to
Permissions, Houghton Mifflin Company, 215 Park Avenue South, New York, New York 10003.

The text of this book is set in 15-point New Caledonia.   The illustrations are watercolor on Arches paper.
Library of Congress Cataloging-in-Publication Data
Rumford, James.
Seeker of knowledge : the man who deciphered Egyptian hieroglyphs / James Rumford.   p.   cm.
Summary: A biography of the French scholar whose decipherment of the Egyptian hieroglyphic language
made the study of ancient Egypt possible.   ISBN 0-395-97934-X
1. Champollion, Jean-Francois, 1790–1832 — Juvenile literature.   2. Egyptian language — Writing, Hieroglyphic — Juvenile literature.
3. Egyptologists — France — Biography — Juvenile literature. [1. Champollion, Jean-Francois, 1790–1832.
2. Egyptologists. 3. Egyptian language — Writing, Hieroglyphic.] I. Title   PJ1064.C6R86   2000   493'.1'092 — dc21   [B]   99-37254   CIP

Printed in Singapore   TWP 10 9 8 7 6 5 4 3

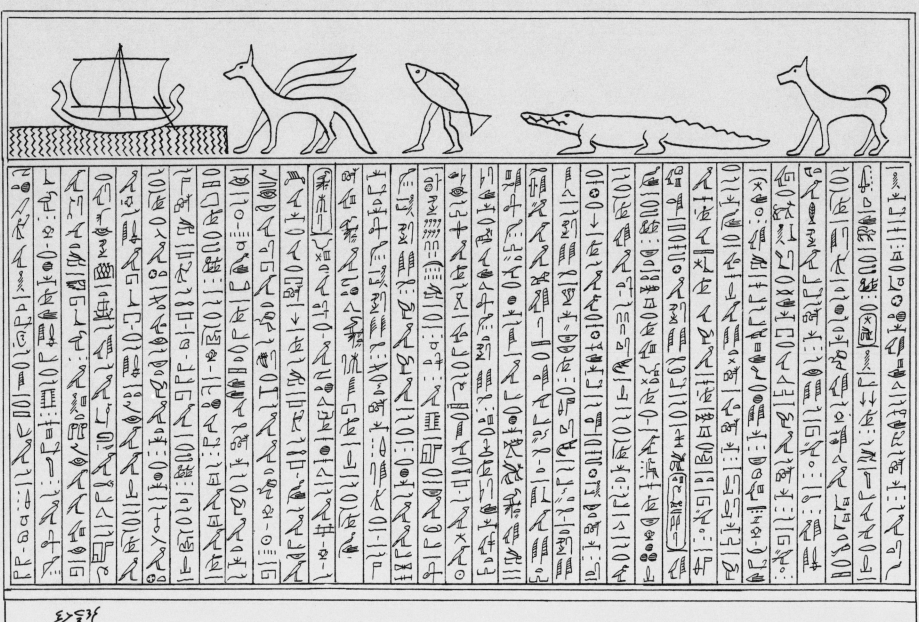